Profane Halo

Lovers in the Used World

Beckon

Tall Stranger

Some Gangster Pain

CHAPBOOKS, LIMITED EDITIONS

Fatherless Afternoon

Woman Speaking Inside Film Noir

THE PLOT GENIE

GILLIAN CONOLEY THE PLOT GENIE

OMNIDAWN PUBLISHING

72 15 129 71 14 128 70 13 127 69 12 126 68 11 125 67 10 124 66 9 123 65 8 122 64 7 121 63 6 180 62 5 179 61 4 178 120 3 177 119 2 176 118 1 175 117 60 174 116 59 173 115 58 172 114 57 171 56 113 70 112 55 169 54 111 168 53 110 167 52 109

Design and composition by Quemadura

Printed offset on acid-free, recycled paper by

Thomson-Shore, Inc., Dexter, Michigan

Omnidawn Publishing is committed to preserving ancient
forests and natural resources. We elected to print this title on
30% postconsumer recycled paper, processed chlorine-free. As
a result, for this printing, we have saved:

3 Trees (40' tall and 6-8" diameter)
1,463 Gallons of Wastewater
1 million BTUs of Total Energy
89 Pounds of Solid Waste
304 Pounds of Greenhouse Gases

Omnidawn Publishing made this paper choice because our
printer, Thomson-Shore, Inc., is a member of Green Press
Initiative, a nonprofit program dedicated to supporting authors,
publishers, and suppliers in their efforts to reduce their use of
fiber obtained from endangered forests.

For more information, visit www.greenpressinitiative.org

Environmental impact estimates were made using the Environmental Defense
Paper Calculator. For more information visit: www.edf.org/papercalculator

Library of Congress Cataloging-in-Publication Data

Conoley, Gillian, 1955–

The plot genie / Gillian Flavia Conoley.

p. cm.

Poems.

ISBN 978-1-890650-42-1 (pbk. : alk. paper)

I. Title.

PS3553.O5144P66 2009

811'.54—dc22

2009030471

Published by Omnidawn Publishing

Richmond, California www.omnidawn.com

(510) 237-5472 (800) 792-4957

10 9 8 7 6 5 4 3 2

CONTENTS

Quick! More lives! ARTHUR RIMBAUD

THE PLOT GENIE

[DRAIN THE POND]

No sound

         then low level jazz . . . then take away

   the jazz—

drain the pond to see the fish.

Or sometimes tortoises, gulls, empty vials of human growth—

maybe a messenger—a slope nosed boxer on a junket

in a satin cape. In an alley—speaking out the side of his mouth—

I am thy father's spirit,

doomed once more and for a certain time

to walk the earth—quipped

Comedy Boy, darkening the door

with his frame,

                  self-advertising.

                 Ashy reek of horsepiss,

   drifting cabbies.

        R drew a letter from his pocket, read it

        once more, and folded it into the newspaper

        he was carrying. Miss Jane Sloan

        had Handsome Dead Man

        on a scrap of paper

        inside her purse.

THE PLOT GENIE

If a person is fawning or obsequious to another.

To remove a tabu, to be rid of carping.

The desire to obtain possession of a key,

insanely jealous love.

We are here to escape payment of a lost wager.

To secure life insurance,

to escape an abomination.

Evening. White sand. A small distant figure, tiny sultan, or a speck

on the windshield stirring.

A natural reality of

white summer of white panes.

Once a handsome dead man was floating on the pool,

white sands' small distant figure

came into view, and you felt a pang of delight

under your skull as we drove on,

speck on the windshield stirring

in white summer

of white panes. Then home

                   to read night's

starry dismemberment

of book,

         Hamlet's

         toque feather

      drifting down

            Mallarme's page,

and come morning,

we were going up to Portland,   backing out the car.

It was day, a moose was sighted in the forest. A bus decayed in its interior,

the palace gate swung shut.

Low, evaporating trails of night terror of what happening. The getting there
of next.

Let me introduce Miss Jane Sloan, head of the department,

and a very capable authoress,

dozing off in an armchair near the window,

near Nature producing

its unidentical designs, the chasm side of a stick of butter.

The plot genie is baking a pan of biscuits.

The plot genie is one of the most virile helps which has ever been devised.

■

Someone is falling into an ancient cave comfort,

barely touching another origin, dialing

a unique number and none other, holding the plot genie in the hollow of
an arm

while careful not to bend, spinning

while out the palace gates trots a horse color of gray, dark splotch.

Soon we are approaching the studios to say,

was it better than a painting, to get even

with someone, to use a colloquialism, in the light

of a game or a sporting event?

In the house of shadows, the shadow of the house.

In the house I hear nothing but laughter,

weaponry, airy plumes on helmets, war relics and attic wasps.

In the dusty corners, parasitical words

having drunk of an antiquity

by whose forces Europe ruled. ·

The house resting blankly

in wintry afternoon curing in the sun

like a little ham. The plot genie's

hand reflected in the lake,

her hand smudged in the flat calm glare.

In a bunk house, underworld

dope den. Back of a music hall,

in a bachelor's apartment. Betty,

then Veronica

meticulously dressed in the margins, Archie

never drawn too quickly, but with patience, exactitude,

in the white rapids he might one day shave from his face, always speaking in the simple human tongues that Sappho kept going, admiring their clarity.

To be free, and 21, to be born into a lush landscape

and to come back to it in a box,

as if in an old evening suit.

The genie tells you what happens and you listen,

as if in repay for the years the swarming locust has eaten.

The genie tells you what happens

and then along come still others to explain. If you still don't get it, the plot
genie repeats.

■

As a child Miss Jane Sloan came upon a diamondback rattler. On a girl scout day camp, s'mores and wieners, old gray sheds, blisters and sunburn, at least one case of bull nettle rash on a bare ass. Motes drifting above weedy path like automata surveying an earlier globe. The diamondback did not rattle. In hot noon sun, pungent sulfur smell of snake, the child body of Miss Jane Sloan alarmingly tangible as she walked backward, nervous spasms beneath her white socks, high grass parting like disinterested third persons standing aside to let her pass, to let her back so far away, just far enough away so she could still see, where. . . . look, there is a wooden bench just strong enough for her to stand on. It was a beautiful sunny day. A peculiar speech signal could be overheard between suspects. I was afraid I was about to permit an unrecognized sister to starve. A relative had decided to jump a bail bond. Part of a body, or a portion of the spoils, was found in the possession of the subject. And Miss Jane Sloan went down. She went down the white road of aftermaths, no Titanic. She went down the alterations of, to the barely beyond, where everything was begging everything to come back to where we live. When Miss Jane Sloan closed her eyes she could feel slight neuronal embraces caving in, tuned to the vibration of other tormentresses. Whatever sulks there. The dust eliminated. Destiny is a world apart.

■

To remove a tabu to be rid of carping   is the desire to obtain possession of a key.

The desire to bring about a reformation   to overthrow authority

is to satisfy an appetite.   The screen is

the desire to produce a phenomenon,   how much everyone needed a glass of water.

We are here to escape   payment of a lost wager.

To secure life insurance   to satisfy a horoscope

to defeat a plot   the river's sheen.

To possess an abode   our virgin torso

to be refused forgiveness   to escape from a master

to get relief from a monstrosity   or abomination.

A line of boxcars   slides open

completely frontal   to escape a carousel.

■

street, door

dark diatomaceous

silver drink

Safe night world

open, long hallway long

bright

shoulder hunch

stairs of crickets

wet bar

wet bar rag

doublecross to

half-hatched plans

time of   redemption and time

to define excess before plummeting

or stuck in a web in wait, with

one-winged bird taunts   ocelot on leash   a vast

grotto, finite infinite infinite finite infinite

hup two three four

wants not to

to say something

something says then wants to

be

something wants

maw

opens

maw

maw

turpitude of tawny fronds of tidepools,

turned away,

characters creeping up the alley, the most non-existent of faces

lit

severally,

A blank photograph arrives in the mail.

What to do with it

like one silk stocking

throughout

the war. Out of wet pools of blotting paper

comes a coal rose.

If with her all of life went by.

Since there was a child with a drum.

Why I interrogated her left-behind straw.

Or the cast-open portal and situation gallow to a realm

of a friend and his friend starting by airplane

on their hunting trip, never to return.

Because the book's oily covers

contain the body they were looking for.

House a-twitch.

Within the welcoming shouts of a far-off companion.

If you read her Chapters on the Atlantic,

or as is said of the dead, she had worn her jacket under your jacket.

Very low down

very high up

the Alone

rolling toward the Alone

along her optic seacoasts

[CULTE DU MOI]

We are captains of fatigue. The sound is an enterprise. Serial balconies along the street. I miss the sound of typing one letter at a time, and many machines typing letters at the time. When I was loping through the yard one day, I felt like Whitman, it was the closest I got to feeling like a man though sometimes in pickup trucks, there was Paul Bunyan. Once under the dappling elms I became two innocent boys who kicked a basketball onto the lawn of the scary man's scary house, and when the scary man came out to chase the boys away whose basketball it was he died of a heart attack he was so angry and unable to speak the basketball, the word basketball, as when you open your mouth and nothing comes. We are captains. So far over 6,000 of us have died, depending on who you talk to. Our bodies are imitations of the spirit and our statues are imitations of imitations, a la Aristotle. Our bodies hang from rafters, magnolias, lampposts and telephone poles. When all has been said, and has been argued to no end, it begins to rain on the pictograph. Our buses reek worse than the people on them, our buses carry us anywhere they are extraordinarily accepting urine reeks but rarely stains when you get down to it you smell it much more often than you see it, unless you look back, and I try to take off my steaming boots. I can't *give away* my sleeping dogs. A pinafore a piano forte a fugue, I got the best job in the world by just being myself and then I fell forward arms lifted into a pause of music arrested in the idea with my eyes closed I am usually happy to do anything for art, but this was a job not a wandering aim. I got it and then I quit so as not to ruin. I tried to tell everyone everything I thought they wanted to hear then I became a captain a fatigue. Once a plagiarist tried to steal me but I ran and ran faster into a tumbling, refreshing stream, then I stood in a long line waiting for bread. Her Lawrence brought his face home still burning to death from the war. No one comes to thank the steam for the engine, no one regards the cow when you can get the milk in fraying grids of lace. I plan the day in finding in Poe a soul-brother by whose insight I might maintain my own different, negress-warmed and orient-colored spirit, a growing boy of uncommon experiences and opportunities. I usually see a house in the distance.

[E AND R]

If you really love me, then let's stand together, off to the side, near

the realities, away from the microphones, and make our troth, Ok?

Ok.

Good. Repeat after me.

I'm gonna love you.

I'm gonna love you.

I'm gonna love you as if you were my last.

Oh, I like that.

You like it? Then say it.

I'm gonna love you as if you were my last under lightly surging curtains

by large invisible windows within the pool's light. Ok?

Ok.

We are dust collection.

We are dust collection.

You shall be deemed guilty of a misdemeanor.

Who shall be deemed guilty of a misdemeanor.

We shall be two events at the same time unbeknownst to any or all who are
watching.

By your hands I can tell you are a traveling man.

You are fully mingled with the one who has your face.

Tigers can help you get out of your predicament.

If tigers can help you get out of your predicament, I'll wait for you in the
first guest house cabin

near the white weatherboard.

Now listen and repeat what you hear to yourself, silently.

A girl sat in the woods feeling lonely and sad.

A bird, who had been watching the girl,

lowered herself to the girl's shoulder, and said,

"Just say nice things to yourself out loud."

It is fun to imagine that you are the turtle on a warm rock. Enjoy breathing.

If the color is red, let it travel up your legs.

Let green explore your temple, blue

may swirl around your forehead, relieving you

of all thoughts.

We may remove our shoes and put our feet in the warm water.

Today we are like the Mongols, heading terrifically westward,

riding horses with our feet.

Today we may remove our shoes and put our feet in the warm water.

Today we pull our blue jeans down from a branch.

Remember Berlin in 1919. Try to remember Berlin.

Cherry tree, hussy, caution tape, one grammy, one daytime Emmy.

Our great bodies, our heads, as a boy sits watching a quiet pond.

His eye seeks yours in an eye-to-eye handshake

and holds it there as before death.

Tigers can help you. You are not a sick individual. Or realm.

The turtle, curious, also puts his feet in the water.

If you really love me,

our great heads, our bodies, conceived in the chasm of a rental car, or a
golden chariot,

before it all flew away.

DEAR E,

Have allowed another foreigner into my soul.
Have received transfer of some letters from a third.

To live by raft down possibilities,
waiting for one's orders—

you will drift here by dawn
you will carry envelope of debris

you will further into oceanic crate chased by axe—
and the clothes that flash on

one leisurely,
and the blood left behind, as if unmopped into a paint can.

I relish sun on deserted village.
Once I stood, once I slept

naked, tools on my belt, as you would
have me—harpies circling the airstrips,

cycling the forest canopy—changing my voice

and head winds. I loved it when you said,

"when they first handed me the dictionary, I thought it was a poem about
   everything."

I understood your mazy way, thus tranced, one hand in the tar pot.

         "It was on a side road outside of Los Angeles.
         I was hitchhiking from San Francisco to   San Diego, I guess.
         A half hour earlier I'd thumbed a ride.
         Well, so long mister, thanks for the ride, the three cigarettes,
         and for not laughing at my theories on life."

         But you broke off right in the middle of a sentence.
         Why do you keep looking for new people,
         New places, new ideas?
         Not worried about your future?

         "Oh, I got plenty of time for that."

That's precisely how antagonists wreck one's mind.
To feel no identity aright except
one first stirred
by becoming someone else—

         which does not so much relieve
         my hunger to become,

as keep it immortal in me—do you not
feel too

      a green sapling's invisible

domineerings?

      The saw blades and leaf blowers,

             the acetylane torchers

    who melt
    the pitch,

         and with one journey finished,
         so begins another, and with another over, so starts

the next, and on, on, into

the long intolerable arc,
no hour of doom to come

     in the still shivering

E,

will you be beside my every hap?

R

DEAR R,

Comedy Boy came by horseback with your letter,

his head appeared then disappeared in woods receding

as he rode
between trees, in chambers dim with histories,

times a shaft of sun would fall on his pale hair
and convert it to silver—

and so I imagine you,

fellow jailbird—stepping as on gilded stepping stone,

with dilated eyes of one who has just come from a dark place

or perfecting machine. Mojave hotel. Laps in the deep end.

Fools ogle in summer. Mattress dries.

E

Comedy Boy was on all fours, like the hours he was about to crumple—he had been looking up questionable things on the internet doing the pornography all afternoon and he was on all fours now, it had been that kind of day, wasted—in his opinion—not even grocery store putting things away just feeling his penis sway and rise then tide to the tits clit ass really long ones stuck in every crevice and now he was on all fours—trying to open himself up to the poem—stars hidden under stars, the moon tasting pretty good, the pornography sparkling but unadorned and fading, the pornography not even something to discuss. The poem was opening and Comedy Boy could feel it —the abstract and the sublime—the ferry arriving to pick Comedy Boy up, and this made him smile. He lashed himself to the mast. It was failed spring. The sound was unfixed, the distance, the shortest. The fog was soon up to Comedy Boy's waist. The fog was like a pause before other weather, leaving before it was leaving. Keats could feel all this in his lungs.

ACROSS BLACK ASPHALT carved
into gum mastics and jungle fern,

if house is meadow, if house is brain,
if long red lies the tide and action is abated,

among others who are
we were trying to quit

the world, and head straight
into larval stage of indigenous waters

on flat raft,
R with golden sickle,

E with moonstruck veil,
burning her card of the old maid—

Comedy Boy was just thinking,
if E and R would get into that dingy

I would no longer have to travel
between them in resinous breath

of cosmicity's piney woods,

as if I am on leash of vestigial
lizard tail!

Redhead wanting
me to dye her eyebrows
and pluck out her mustachios,

Handsome Dead Man
rising in room after room
lighting cigarettes room
after room, Handsome Dead Man

giving a small laugh,
saying things like, "I'd
like to show you

I'm not talking out the back
of my neck," laughing

in the sunshine,
in a tired-looking raincoat,

in the excellency of going on, in a tired-looking raincoat,

R: You mean we can't win?
E: No, we can't win.

Handsome Dead Man, giving a small laugh, in a tired-looking raincoat.

"I'd like to show you I'm not talking out of the back of my neck," before a glass-fronted building,

in the sunshine,

in the raincoat,

pensive,

       A man goes to the doctor and says, Doc, I'm not feeling so well.

       Ok, the doctor says, I want you to tell me a typical day, what you do

       from the minute you wake up to the minute you go to bed.

       "Well, I wake up and I vomit, and then I

       "Whoa. Wait, wait a minute.

       You do what? You wake up and you vomit?"

       "Yeah.

       Doesn't everybody?

"I'd like to show you I'm not talking out of the back of my neck,"

All   those   people   they   put   in   the   deathhouse.

THE DEATHHOUSE

       Hey Doc here comes the DA

[MELODRAMA]

Try to imagine a long steady hand steering the ocean liners

I am hit on, with good letterhead

and the walls chat,

Miss Jane Sloan seen walking before long umbilical mirrors in corridors
of hotels

The prairies go for miles out here

Floors have inkjets

Miss Jane Sloan is a very well-dressed man and the cold air is whipping
her legs

She has no corset for the page

the pages seething

[MISS JANE SLOAN]

Once they manufactured the studio, I gave out.

The precise words I used that afternoon.

Long Parable of the Hairpin Bend . . .

> as in oils
> as in oil cloth

and what they couldn't do with a computer!   roars in the roars in halls

wet whistles in the teeth of the comb

> in the prairies, breakfast gongs,

> the kind that so please the horsemen—

You may think I am taking too much credit in relating this small episode.

As for Handsome Dead Man, who taught him his songs, I do not know.

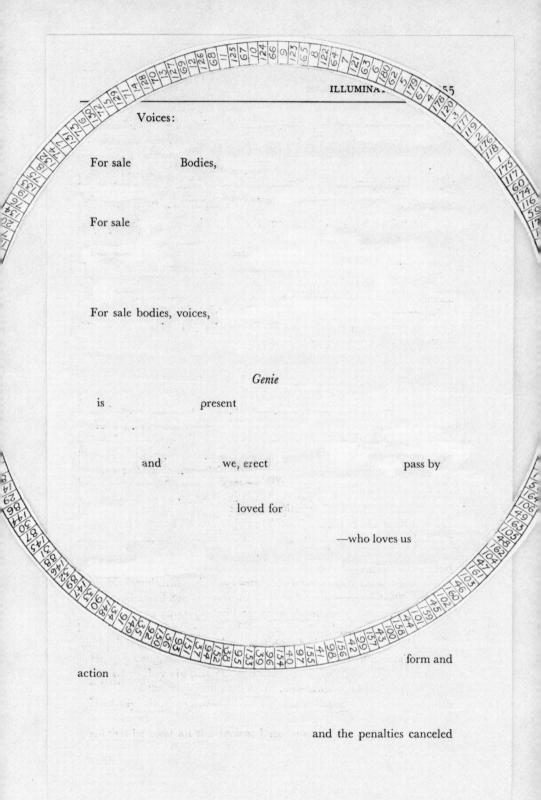

Voices:

For sale   Bodies,

For sale

For sale bodies, voices,

                    Genie

is   present

        and   we, erect   pass by

            loved for

                    —who loves us

                                        form and

action

                    and the penalties canceled

WORDS DIE, THE WORLD IS ETERNALLY YOUNG,

says Aleksei Kruchenykh,

dying in 1968, the year we were beating the year
with a little axe:

1968- 1968- 1968- 1968.
Many of us were not there, but were rumored soon to arrive.

If you believe, moonlight through the window at each landing, the planet looping
the distant waves.

The world is a weird luminescence.
A greenish glow, unhinged.
It is unruled by a dowager, an empress, a madonna, a lopped-off head,
    a great red disc.

We lay sleeping in the arborvitae
and cypresses and ferns,
unsurprised and semi-conscious, not knowing
which is more fictional—the hand in the book,
or the book in the hand.

All-powerful nudes stepping into showers
our bodies a series of planes
best rendered in oils—
we are not untouched
by Modernism, though to stay modern is too much work.

Most ideas have their secret motives.
The earth has its arenas
cross-cutting on top, under, inside, combusting far away into a space probe.

The future is a probe, tied to its fear
of stopped time, or the half memory
of a kind of cyber hell

in which we fled the hedged passage.
Sunspun the bureau for the fleece of gold.
Or all is forever
created and creaturely—

a multiverse
without a manual
in which someone who is not you,
but an exact replica of you, is holding a book

in a room or a public space or a mode of transport that is not where you are,
but is an exact replica of where you are,

on an earth which is not the earth
but an exact replica of the earth
on which you stand
as if on an uninhabited plain,
and it is not a distancing to compare
not a photo not an image
and there doesn't seem to be direction though there is wind,

there is no time but the light remains.

No one is weaving a great shroud
and no one is unweaving a great shroud
but the weave is present because it is
thought about and the weave is taut.

If you look, I have turned
to face your shore, and have come from far away
composing a path of words or word thread

in which perhaps we share a hope for others
even if they are half dead and lying between us,

we recognize them in their shredded clothes
in the tin types or live feeds and reach out
to wipe their brows, not there, thin air—

Sunlight piercing oxygen
clean through we are imagining again that we are no one and
every variety of nuisance of no one

and so we are kind of
allied

and following a conversation
made as we are of molecules and lament
where an intelligence lives.

And whether I am on the replica of that intelligence,
or on the intelligence itself,
it is no matter,

we stand as if on an uninhabited plain,
and it is not a distancing to compare

not a photo not an image
and there doesn't seem to be direction, though there is wind,

there is no time but the light remains
and you do not look back.

AGENTS OF ETERNITY, they never

call you at home, Circe says, pouring her animals

honey and wine. Pages

make good windows, blindfolds,

plates of glass altering dissonances,

instances, unled choirs—

let us leap down to the tossed boats below.

Is the journey not royal?

Have you not seen our pursuers?

Why are you out on the frozen lake alone milady?

I was out by the fire, but the others left me behind.

A ROSE FOR A ROSE, a dog in the yard

says to a dog in the yard, who says precisely,

and a panther's cries are like glinting shards

of sun shuffling the river, especially if you

try to think of the government without the

government lens. I thought it was a conceptual

piece to walk up and shit upon

said the dog in the yard to the bent figure,

who then whispered it to the name Lord,

then to the tired automaton working his gait,

working his high color, striking a match

along his zipper. All the doo-da day.

Are you in a state of grace? Be careful,

it's a dangerous answer, urged Artaud,

speaking to Joan.

[R O M A N C E]

inharmonious red stars   satellites not even stars   over a line of taxis

(extend your hand, extend your hand, bring me high words and locusts
    without end
dormant ((someone has to take over))

like the two drinking the last of their alcohol in the apartment

two sleeping it off later

one rolling over calm as a ballast— slow glissando of a muscle group
    caught under sheets

porch swing in— wind in didn't we need
the rain— the swing in— rain

forcing the earth to smell the earth, the dung of the two

sleeping in

in what anyone will do next, springing tiger

[MY NAME IS THE GIRL WITH ONE GLASS EYE SAID BITTERLY]

My name is the girl with one glass eye said bitterly.

                                        Nightingale

in the birdfeeder hung from the pepper tree opening throat to the body

of light in (was it spring?)

                    spring's shipwreck—

high voices. lank hounds

ramping it up over a highway arcing out into empty air—

where we

were resiliencies at the edges of time

dining on upended peach crates—

on lawn chairs dropped into the shaded pool

of the bottomless–where through the murk

Muses and Mediums regenerate the pool's Elysian scum. I am the girl who

    opens the seashell

that stirs the cauldron

that sings us back to the leafy path witch-worn and cobbled thru—

What do you walk upon?

Something already

in the blood.

What line of work you in?

job is Job is Job is job is Job it's all part of an infinite

series foci aperture

$2/3$ $3/4$ $1/8$ scherzo   pattern I get it,

you look like someone I used to know

drinking out of a garden hose.

Can we summon by the hooks in the water

all the broken—as in the belly of an unsuspecting

mother—can we open the open

the hatchback to hear the Gothic echoes—a virgin forest asway amid the

    Giant's sperm?

Tomb for Tit,

come, wounds— extension cords carried to a midnight execution and left

to dangle there, a beheadedness played over

and over culture soaking it up   I knew a Garden:

meaning of the world is the intaglio of   it's sunny and 75.

What do you walk upon? Something already in the blood drafts an ink,

reconstitutes the flowers. Do you feel a light in the sun

on your back, piercing through the water, it's a light—said the said the I

am the girl with one

glass eye said

bitterly, now let me go, she said, holding the flowers to

long opal tails of moon waving slowly

from time to time

saying No no no no no no no, I am

the girl now that we are on the page of infinite

length,

in the city of uplanded height, on the lawn of rising

green   in the alley tunneled

down to a chambered core,

and I said how many people did you see on the road rolling up their old kit bag

how many people did you see

trying to get where trying to get there

trying to see the many people you have seen on the road

under the star's starkness under the exits entranced

under the mistral of

rain

feeding the lengthening stream we step into—out of —shuttering—

    pictured there

FREQUENTLY, Handsome Dead Man
knew a way out. Faint blue nightlights
as on a runway of black rubber matting.
E, he'd call out, then R,
he'd hoot softly. Each
would arrive to follow him along
the corridor, and once out of sight,
they would anoint themselves with oil,
making the wild beast, almost naked,
just a scrap or two from costume,
for when they were called back.

THE MANDATE TO STOP the funding
required people of complete
unthinking panic though not torchbearers
themselves. In low stretches of night,
Redhead fencing money in a cream-colored
Lincoln. "We could try not to exist
or come fully to speak the word
within this world." *Well, that's a goal.*
"Bitches and ho's, please just try
to mark this one more clearly
for the printer." *Me, for instance,*
I'm the daughter of a Marine
who wept in front of the television
"if you want to be in television
just crack it open and sit there,"
he said, smoking his Winstons.

HER LONG DIAPHONOUS gown cast across the variables

and vanishing points where for

further foliage, lake, day,

her method was moths stuck to a wall,

her method the balcony where we wait.

sit wait. sit to wait.

Color made everyone stare

into the long anarchy before them.

Beauty induced by other women

for men when they were drunk was induced

by Greta Garbo when they were sober.

Conciousness felt flayed. Conciousness

wiped its face of its own fog—stretched—and sank back

on its haunches. The genie

was the first to think of elongating everyone.

[B R A D   A N D   A N G E L I N A]

To have to not have the actors get acquainted before (they shoot)

so awkwardness
of two characters feels like

awkwardness of two characters in marriage therapy

makes good disturbance in the field
genius on director's part both

hired assassins
unbeknownst to each other

assigned to kill each other
is marriage

"I've missed you,
honey"

lit metropolis is writing
and could get to be event

if Brad and Angelina
would just get out of the way of tiny pinholes in the social mindscape

Angelina's critiqueless good thighs
making fine urban murals

"Papadaddy, you comin to me now!"
Angelina occurring

Brad floating by no time even
high and dry it is best

to be the subject, not just about it,
a kind of prayer one utters silently

then enters like Angelina's faint vagina musk
Brad's sheep-a-leaping

Why do they walk the walk
and talk the talk that they are taller than we are
their heads brush the rain

The voice tells us *Brad's seaside villa,*
the faint vagina musk the penis smoothness enormity
of places, people, and things

To dare to put your own hands on your own hips
and stroke her shoe horn,
the breathless breasts and wild rock the Brad

that is the equal of the cliff head of cheat grass
the hinged panels of the human hand

Unpeopled climbs the steeple, a pulley-system,
Angelina's lips parting and coming together again in a scarlet lake

in the expanding of time
by the internal

proliferations of oriental
storytelling
a clown shaking his own hand and slapping his own butt

                                                    "Say,

          ,   ever been

                              in this part of the country
                              before?" inquires Brad,
                              huge smoke-drag trailing
                              out of his nostrils

as a bloody murderess hobbles out of her Ramcharger into the vet clinic
to loot supplies for her wounded leg
giant grasshopper
lighting on the white hood of the Ramcharger

gold sun
on the grasshopper's tough and pliant
breast plate

Would you rather

a. love an enemy

b. dream of dishonor of a loved one

c. exhibit fatal ambition by duty to country

d. talk crops or play jackknife

asks the half-clad native girl, resolutely placing her spear into the mud,
so that all night long a rain falls down and refreshes the field.

[F R A N K E N S T E I N]

I, too, would like to know why
I should like to speak to you again of the sea,

or at least hear again in the time before,
first the social body was alive and warm.

Psyche giving birth to her child Bliss—
those were the days when I was in my ass form.

A dragon's purse,
exhausting work in my day.

Something and Nothing

arguing with my master, all because her descriptions were dying—

The other day Something was up and walking around
for an instant,
not realizing it was Nothing—

(how stupid can they be?)

Something and Nothing on the road

the blood flowing   the oxygen flowing
over dandelions and spiders

Something and Nothing
dead tired before their blocks of solitaire

the green banks
the icy hut upon the mountain

their wandering hands rowing my being

Readers still to come

[K I N D L E D]

Kindled pieces of sun
clanging broken upriver

Comedy Boy listing slightly to the side,

one hand blocking piercing sunrise one hand
peeling out,

truck stirring gravel dust
pure lips three priors he comes

with velcro pocket for the cell
leaves topaz greasy headspot on armchair
                                        or sofa

In a pockmarked overstocked functionary neighborhood
one woman kept crawling out the window to avoid the neighbors

and the dinner invitations
vibrating behind them

in the bathrooms
silver hounds
of the faucets
above the marble slabs

Wild tribes were meeting
some slip on the streetcorner

"Try to be there
around six,"
announced Miss Jane Sloan,

straining the cords in her neck

lifting a proverb
up to the morning sun

before putting her hands back into the computer
and feeling around.

[PRETEND YOU DON'T KNOW ME]

Miss Jane Sloan attending
close her prose ignoring all else   hypnotized by the silent vibrato   it
made in her throat.

Handsome Dead Man thinking I must get away from her.
I must return to my personal torture.

My personal torture   is not your personal torture
and for this I hate you more.

In the tink tink of the café, spoon vibrato,   forks clanging politely the china
the porcelain, formica and wood,   chit chat

twittering under sudden outbursts
of laughter—
the happiness of this world they can not get all of it into

a can—
the international language
of the mouth,
the immense thing of

how can someone sit right next to you and pretend
they don't know you

how can you all the years
you have carried
your boxes of literature

from one apartment to the next
pretend
you don't
know me

says Handsome Dead Man out of his
so-called body   in the house Miss Jane Sloan has   in mind to build

pretend you don't know me

with your checkered cloths and coffee mugs

your blush of the apple   in the phantasmagoria

unstirred
in which

we take the morning air

[SHORN POLECAT, THE HELPING VERB FOR WHICH ONE MUST KEEP ONE'S EARS LOW]

We had a taste for celebrity and had once bitten fame.

Along the lower serifs of the city,

a long red scarf to represent temptation.

Why do new poets want to gather round dead poets

and sing?

Oh, it's like chivalry, some would say,

the walnuts falling hard on the roof.

Human, a welcoming figure opening up the melon, making cole slaw of
the important passages.

Wild parrots in the palms of their western city.

From the widow's peak, an outlawish look-see.

The effigy, inlaw, dry leaf, fresh paint, dry rot smell of the old paperback.

In the real world there are no real maps, clippety clop.

      A damp and moldy proof.
Living and dying we lay waste.
~~And~~ sit down ~~to it~~
~~And~~ for a spell.

under shade of porch
                a respite

DEAR R,

In trees
babies come
as in a vision.
Babies howl
as in
good neighborhoods
to make you
wonder.
Living
is a higher thing
than you or I
had dreamed.
The voices
they have
made me
once inside,
explain.

E

DEAR E,

I try the manhole
when I can.
I leave
the manhole
when they see.
The voice is low
today.
My clothes
of a correct era.
Inside my case
I carry you,
though you
don't know.
The tires squeal,
enlarge in heat.
The wind obeys.
The day produces days.
It's been awhile
since makeup came.
The fight jets
bomb only seconds
after we're told.
I know
my part, don't know
anymore. What
you read
we have forgotten.
What I have forgotten
I read and read.

R

Speaking without tones,
wearing without colors,
walking the road walking the road,

when desperate, E tried to sell her enchantment.

[H O W   W E   W I S H]

how we wish   E & R could arrive   in the same story

overlap a red taffeta dress   a cutaway coat   be all   across the lit ballroom

floor— no R

in his sharp-shoulder   high-style tweed coat

fine   specimen of a man   bearing a bunch of roses

through a maze   of busses   cloud

haze,   which bus— no E

in a fluorescent   restroom

pulling up her   shock of brown hair   good for

trailing story's wind   for playing earnest young

woman with uncertain future or   wrapped up as head of surgery

E   shoving open the weighted door   to the hospital's

crystal stairs   how we wish   our faces   would continually   refresh among the chosen,   never the same   habituation of face

inside our heads, the cinema   outside our heads, the cinema

our pure eyes   on the ring of return

how we wish one moment could set them even   feet steady on the ground

retouching   into footprints   we come to life again   like flowers in water

indexically,   potentially,   we look,   and pass—

[DO WE]

do we really need words to stay within the sentence
especially when it is not a long tradition, either

it is an exquisitely
painful way to continue

to stand
in that cut,

changing our shape
utterly in the similarly deadly intimacy, staggering the imagination

western sea, western sea, a thought stream and a fantasy need, western
    sea, western sea

will you be my shapeless nonentity under the ancient olive tree

TYGER

Tyger, one paw curled under, the other splayed out

Sphinx-like

Jungles forget their laws systems their systems

Pronouns like to flee   he who she me

Be pieces in our hands

Making protoplasts and grasslands,

More lives, see how they square

Tyger having drunk of human hormones in spilled lake

Tyger rearing on hind legs a blurry fracas walking straight,

Tyger jumping across rooftops, the storylines played out

In shots of lights, silhouettes crosshatching

In dark windows, the fire-breathing lakes.

Tyger flying over couples in their birthday suits

And deathwear, sunbonnets, shrouds and towels,

Humans punching numbers with stubby fingers in scanned light,

Cashback, hello, wassup, a wail of train and forest parting, Tyger

In a smear of black and yellow stripes

Chasing above the naked, the goddamned and golden armed

Black revolvers out car windows

Tyger in the faint blue nightfalls

Streets scooped out in fearful

Liquefaction to the stripes, the better butter.

blacksmiths

castles

legends

storm

the joy of the new work,

phantoms

mountains

vigils I owed   !

I responded

eyes torn out,

into the room.

A generation tired of its head which understands everything.

Stein drinking her oolong.

Tyger licking his paws, biting his tail.

Dear Plot Genie:

how much longer until someone bursts open,

someone done reading your book and obeying you

[HITCHCOCK]

Could we get by on a polytonic breeze, an aery charm?
A blonde sinking fathoms in the earth?
Could the convertible turn jade
along dreams and dream cliffs growing quiet and magnificent things,
such as night again, day again.
A silent forest ranger had been assigned him.

Bonds falling off
which hold one tethered to the ground,
we are free to dominate the valley like a master.
Slow curve of the earth
as if held by a small boy
on his way to school, the sun
perched on high,
not too far away.
Stairs lead up. A red scarf lands there.
A suitcase opens to a bus station.
Who wants to go back to that terrible time,
everyone smiling discretely, as though forgetting about the war?
Pale kimono in the closet in case we had got blasé
about death being loose in us.

So our lives are spiral staircases spiraling
avid and previous
with kills on either wayside.

Is this scary?

On the edge of the world a long line of black trees.

He wore a pink nosegay to his social skills class.

Winds gusting in the northwest.

We listen to one another breathe.

[SAM FULLER]

I am thinking of my future in a suitcase of champagne.

Door to door traveling black wash/white palette I have

big brushstroke I breathe underneath.

Staggering back from the slap I talk Big Daddy.

I'm still your sister under the hairy foliage.

Après retrieving French peasants from a Nazi cave,

the dogs they are sleeping and the children

are fed, heads bobbing in the backseat.

Human asleep in the sound booth,

crack of this pinecone, those rocks—

swish-swish of dark trousers of twilight—

white seagulls on the black jet

beach, your mother wasn't home

you walked to the sea

[C A S S A V E T T E S]

Black hairdo moved in the frame for the question.

What's that inky noon what's that incarnation?

I don't need God to talk to, I need someone with skin on, says the man in
    the T-shirt,

something enumerated like a phone bill or the Bill of Rights

on the bedside table.

Out the window a midday glare of lampposts and fenders.

In black and white we are ruby-throated

on the white mattress of dishevelment, thinks the man in the T-shirt,

but he doesn't say it. Likewise,

you gotta seek love in a desperate city, says the woman

wordlessly in the black hairdo,

sending the whole heat of her love to the man in the T-shirt, and this without shamefacedness.

When you get there, phone, says the man in the T-shirt, lighting a cigarette
   and waiting.

Jazz, not some deep-dust hillbilly record.

Completely un-mental pieces of time falling on them

in the water tap drip, two

on the edge of the bed drinking and smiling and laughing and walking

to the mirror at the start of the room, actions

beginning within them, actions about to begin.

Actions saying let's go,

as they adjust their clothes and comb their hair, carelessly

down the napes of their necks,

heads huge on the wall,

bent victims of love, undying shades to say the words from.

Dear Master,

I am the master.

[TENDERNESS OF THE DOVE]

Like a vulture to a graveyard.

Like a Brueghal to a red or a Guernica to a black or a Krasner to a hot orange.

Air vague, and best to know it than to not,

And revolution, at least half human soul my brethren scores of death.

Satan knew this about existence and its eves.

Thought is the flowing tap of error and perception,

A voting moron before a neutral ph

Paper, medium surface suitable for pencil, crayon or pastel.

Or what if before sunset we start to drink.

And oil breasts and groins and let loose all other genitalia.

River river river well river river river well

Kitten down the,   rope asway,

Post-crime hands in the sub-daylight   distended joy!

Why in the trees one bird should disabuse another

As one drives past them.

As one's neighbors yank palms from the earth

So the rat can no longer live there.

As one drives on

But yields no power, no ultimate authority,

But is only *apparent* as the birds close up the hole, as the birds cohere.

E: I feel actuated, living on the ends of the earth.

R: What is waiting? And for what do we wait?

E: I've got a better question. What are we walking on?

R: Is this tile real?

E: It's pretty thin.

R: It's no big deal.

E: As long as we don't whack it.

[IT WOULD BE GOOD IF

WE HAD A MESSAGEBOX]

It would be good
if we had a messagebox

but we have only a
"repetition compulsion"

For ex. once I woke up
and Handsome Dead Man

was lying in the bed next to me

End to end and semi-automatically we rose, strode forth
like we were the whole earth together

We swung from a rope

      into a murky pond

we made light of a raid

      of his flattering offers

Someone wanted to inveigle him of his disease genes

Someone wanted
to discredit him of his stronghold

starve him of his air supply

One day
        he was just a man

                  · Ras
                putin

tying his shoelace

                (deep glowful eyes

                almost counterfeiting nature)

      a Hun in a blank photograph

a Marine getting a discharge

then I saw it: this world

empty

of the men supply

■

Redhead was knocked
into the middle of next week

She was

    leaving

a task   a duty
unperformed   unfinished

    She
was suspected
of crookedness

A friend
stood in the way

    blocked by inclement weather

    so long
    so long

a girl with a red cape on horseback

galloping into a forest galloping in

∎

When E
had a chance
to turn around,

she was sweeping a slaughterhouse
pretty dead-end

trying to
make with the regular
appointments

when centuries
fill

the mind

in

it's a big town for

possible
imprisonment

and
shopping

        invasion of a field   a page is an escaped

hospital
    of experience   visibility

a viability

    of grass
    in the leaves' wet

       Leo
        pardi's

back
curved high

over his
    infinitely

skeptical hill, its sighs and plaints

  we follow him down

out of the doleful city

Paradise
    I feel
        more at ease

in

    interstitial tissues
of

the mental circuits
that capture

        and link

Paradise

      I feel
      ease

into the iris
of Tyger

it would be good
if we had a messagebox

DIVISION 7

BUILDING A PLOT

Now I am going to let you do the thing that you have been wanting to do—the thing that is closest to your heart. You are going to build a plot from an outline that I am going to give you. Your conscious mind is beginning to be organized. You have studied the fundamentals of dramatic plot construction, are familiar with the various elements of ingredients that are necessary in a story plot. If you have not thoroughly grasped the difference between Problems, Obstacles, Complications, Predicaments and Crises, I want you to go back over the preceding divisions and study some more. If necessary, choose words from the dictionary and experiment with them. Or you may try this: Look around you and observe various objects (which have names) and see how you can scheme to use them in a plot as problems, obstacles, efforts, etc.

Observe that I said "objects that have names." Right here I am going to quote a famous psychologist who confirms what I have told you about words suggesting ideas—no matter whether you take them from the dictionary, the newspapers or if you simply look at a thing and think of its name and of words that suggest ideas regarding how it could be employed to play a part in a plot. You may find yourself thinking out loud, or talking to yourself, but don't worry. That is not always a sign of insanity.

Doctor Albert Edward Wiggam, who wrote a feature for many newspapers entitled "Let's Explore Your Mind," asks the question, "Is it possible to think without using words?" and then he gives this answer: "Yes, only it is thinking of a very low order. A chimpanzee

[REDHEAD LEAPING OVER THE CLASSIC EXAMPLES TO BE BORN]

Redhead leaping over the classic examples to be born

Redhead climbing the ship in the bottle
and waving widely
inside the bottle at the other phenoms

Bloodletting superstore big gulp C-sectioning
anxiety clouding outside

where the other trains were at their stations
saying *take me take me take me* to another

life you will see other stations

birds birds birds

           grass grass grass

Gabled roofs Eichlered ceilings
heated floors Redhead

                is a young girl,
              she gets on her bike

and rides up the street

daffodils

buttering the way

to the ghost of a ramshackle café:
people hurting themselves with more work

order such small plates   Hyperborean

monkey jackets
pacing up and down the neo-

Babylonian cineplex,
each entire

nerve center, Am I   speaking to a computer?
Am I   that obvious?

Redhead's only companion, the great bird,

bald-faced and corn-fed
linking station to station

The stations

The well-lit well-funded highly-managed tubes
speeding under earth

The paperbacks

saturated from the human oils

Redhead entering the one just opened (American reprint, circa 1940's),

Redhead full-bodied among the pages we don't have time to read

and winter came, and spring arrived.

"We're all nuts!" Tom had said, with a feeling that he had at last
discovered the great fundamental truth.

"You're god-damn right!" Mahoney had replied.

"Ever hear of Karkow?" Caesar Gardella had asked an hour later.

No no, this is bigger than that

island in the post-whirl of things to spawn the O2

Redhead woke feeling a little pseudoexperienced

Then peeled herself away

from time

and re-inserted herself

     into a clean break

Got to get away from MASTERPIECES

stacked up

and walking alongside her about the same height but opposed

to LIFE, she thinks

     no one sits long in the THRONES OF CREATION

the agent is carbon

comes a coal rose   a colossi

    a saxifrage gleans wild in the rock cliff, a curl
lets loose

    down the moist nape of a neck

                a chignon

if house is meadow
if house is brain

lighting flowers
with a little butane

                          we make with the jokes

brief things

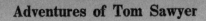

'It's blood, it's blood, that's what it is!' over and over

Everything was swimming

frequently slipped the bandage free afterward slipped the bandage back to its place again.

It
get done

in all

void
said nothing;

grated

jail-window
through
The jail
marsh

was seldom occupied.

The
Injun

could be
the matter,

the grave
deemed wisest not to try

[A CLUSTER BOMB

A CLUSTER HEADACHE]

A cluster bomb a cluster

headache, a catatonia of elm.

In the motor orders of the

mockingbirds and thrushes

a memory of a memory stood a chance, the way

we remembered it

a church burning down.

Dispatch of sheets

of dark plastic sheets

over weeds suffocating for months,

bewitched female mass.

Three little fishes two loaves of bread.

How many days before someone bursts open

someone done reading your book and obeying you

cream in commonlight

white walking man

drying triptych of motor oils.

Redhead ethical in her

sit bones in blue jeans against bare bench

pine needles scrape cheek a medication

in which one unbinds.

In the later future in the dominant form of future

Comedy Boy in the aisle also serves and waits in a desert place.

A boy with one girl's hand

and one boy's hand,

an agony and a green updraft.

"How sorry I am!

to

be

forced to live there!—

you are all of you dif-
ferent creatures; you do not look

well at present."

or

entirely free

you will think better

altogether,

"What is the matter, sir?—Did you speak to me?"

"I am sorry my father   does not think you

succeeded in the true English style,

a calmness

conversible,

Emma

, always the greater talker.

local information

could not fail

The plan of a drain,

spring corn

to inquire about,

a little gruel."

the sea air."

they had all taken their places,

close to her.

insensibility   sat

at her elbow,

admiring her drawings

like a would-be

lover,

all would yet turn out right,

in the most over-powering

Now, it so happened

MARCH ORDERS.   Orders march.

When we walk, one thigh rubs another.

Britches. Petticoats. The sackcloth of hair,

a fig tree swollen with untimely figs. The dispatched car,

the one window down, the World Music failing the world's (untrained) voice.

To the brigands and the demigods, to the Brahman and the Hottentot,

to the Rolands and the Mabs, the Vision lengthened and gathered.

French beauties. Italian models, live birds in the high wigs.

The canal drizzled. Trials terminated. Lots changed. Our bodies.

ONE COGGED CIRCLE fits
the many wheels revolve a turbid wake
spiralizes

the mariner and the genie

hand in hand

"Truth is a pathless land." —Jiddhu Krishnamurti

"Only when there is no path and no procedure
can you get to The Way." —Chuang Tzu

"There is a goal but no way; what we call a way is hesitation."
—Kafka

Truth is: anyone can make a sign, all you need is paint.

Rimbaud: "Having arrived   at all times, you'll depart on all sides."

no treading in one's own footsteps,
no turning back the blobs of gum

"When cornered there is a change; when there is a change, there is a
passing through. There is always some kind of way out." —Hisamatsu

"You can float in it, fly in it, suspend in it
and today it seems, to tremble in it
is maybe best or anyhow
very fashionable." —Willem de Kooning

THANKS VERY MUCH BUT I HAVE TO SEE A MAN ABOUT A HORSE.

A pickup stalled in a rain gully. Aimless horses, munching.

A dog's bark growing more distant in the hills.

TV portions playing in the head of the joy-faced

autistic boy running up and down the bank.

E and R and P and Q and L and M.   E and R full of ardor.

P and Q divorcing,   L and M, never making it.

■

And I?

Circling your hologram

wanting back the hideous statement

that so hurt your self esteem. I am so sorry.

This is where the real people

met all the actors and actresses

until everyone broke down and cried

tears into the apertures

and life went on.

The scapula, the femur. The pelvic floor.

E and R attaching themselves to the page as to a sail

and hoping to blow into the real.

■

To the room there. To the making room there. Unclassifiable.

The page emptying of E and R,   the creek shoal   shifting pebbles in the glint of white spruce sun.

The page

returning to its

hunger.

[P A R A D I S E]

It is hard to be at the right funeral.

Sometimes two columns form.

Some like to think of Beckett, some like to think of Williams, each

with a typewriter, returning.

The funicular and the nightingale

and the closed rooms we like to indulge them in.

A submissiveness.

A white heron, angular and hard, watching from the top of the tree, watching the water and the waste.

No vertigo along the tracks—as one car creaks up, the other goes down,
    faceless.

The heron taking off and landing, then awkwardly turning away, refusing
    to move.

NO ONE TELLS you like it is. I think it was warm that day. Sound and pulse the whales spouting such imaginary languages, chime and time and slap be lie we woke on deck not slaves, not surrogates, the atmosphere unfurled to what most could recall before the rains, the every several gates. I think it was warm that day we did not stay inside dimensional limits of "natural selections," the marryings/buryings/buzzing cries—but sensed the prelingual in the nearly dead, and felt with each sun the limp limbs of the just woken nodding "yes" to the Yes—I think we were pedalling by a busted screen door somewhere in the house slamming back and forth in the scent of jasmine and dried plums—germination, maturation, rot—the river urging us, the returns of the four winds knocking aside the machines and all along the burning eye   the instant of meaning   the hide seeks of Tyger

UNSCROLL to four
Japanese women in kimonos, gazing
into a pond, four white-dusted
faces looking back at the ones on the
wooden bridge. Floating fans. Reading
along the lines, the eye vanished. Since
no wagon was coming that day, we abhorred
wagons. The eye opened. Handsome Dead Man
was collapsed across a piano
in the Alps. Snow broke forth. Water
rose. Monster homes courting the asp,
we descended each flight of steps.
They were renting the trenches. The
dogs were to go in the caves. The dogs
read for a while, then went to sleep
on the newspapers. Unknown soldiers killed
unclaimed soldiers, together at last.

SOLITUDE, meet Deep.   Solitude, don't blow my head to bits.

Nausea Rat's
furry head spinning on the phonograph, floating by just then, on a standing
    order.

Dear Plot Genie:
Siren is done reading your book and obeying you.

Siren is in a flag skirt climbing a most architectural black hearse,

drawn by eight black horses, sable plumed. A thunderstorm

split, water groaned then gave way then gushed
into the sewers—

where Miss Jane Sloan, Redhead, E, R, and you

were there—meaning a shot was heard, and then the long
nothing.

Many thought we were leaving a railway station, but soon
it was as if we had set sail

on a gray sea, with a long ground-swell
such as Solitude remembered

from Old Castille. Repeatedly a stationmaster returned to despair
before the station, where a newly formed boy

leapt into life's rick-shaw, searching
the ram, the dipper, the archer—forgetting again how he was framed.

Redhead appeared before grated jail window
in paneled gloomy room,
and soon someone began to talk.

Trouble, o trouble, trouble,
Blurry Gesture of Countless Fingers
picked up the phone.

They did not have a sofa, so they sent us to the chair,
said Handsome Dead Man.

Death to come of Redhead's
prepared speech
as her eyes cast searchingly

for her prepared speech— *Easy, easy* said the paperback
writer, then Redhead rose

to complete the scene's sleight of hand
in sapling pines. Siren returned a flag skirt.

Impolite to stare.
Worse to point.

Finitude, perpetuity, bareback, spectra. A temporal span, said The Cipher,
    is what I like, a nether-sided

chalky slate.
A gaunt figure in an uncitified occasional rain.

Redhead's desire was like a sunset

piercing her hands,
an afflicted casket of jewels,

but few could attend
that huntscape. A cipher in the sky. A cipher opened upon second mention.

A packed suitcase has such promise.

Trouble, o trouble, trouble,
Blurry Gesture of Countless Fingers
picked up the phone.

Handsome Dead Man heard
the crepitations of the fire,

and again the hurried beatings
of his own heart, as against a terrible

and lovely hush of all
created life. *Then take me with you.*

—Everything has been arranged, R says, we will just let the world implode!

E: If today I am a countess, I will take from my work table
   the gold case that you have given me, open it, and offer you some cigarettes.

R: Or how 'bout you be "tree" and I'll be "homeland."

E: The coin in my hand turned out to be bacteria's jellied cytoplasm.

R: If today we are a summer's night in one besotted mind.

E: Let's not speak, especially when there is no scope for words.

R: But I listen for your whisper as fog lifts when sun begins!

E: Sshh!!

R: You, who have sold whole provinces into the mainstream.

E: Who ain't a slave?

R: Tomorrow you will be led by spruce boy toward a threshold.

E: Princes, pundits, everywhere a prince.

R: Ssshhh! I hear footsteps! Who's coming? I hear invading forces!

E: Quick, we must lie on the divan as though we have never moved from there.

R: No— Let us stand in clear sunlight with no more
   wavering in the face than in the next statue's.

—The whole roadstead was white with foam.—

[SOUND OF FREEWAYS DIRECTING THE COSMOS BACK TO ITS START]

Death's got some spiraled plenitude in the distance between clocks,

both a velocity and a stasis at large. A fly curves its legs in

dioptrical, tense moments of rest on the window sill.

Try not to stare

at the white tiles in a urinal

and think what are you

doing here postcard face

postage stamp face

both believing and disbelieving

a harder time can come, which keeps believing around.

In the amniotic first few

    moments of the film arrive the windshields

we can move in,

hot cold color smears of full-length

characters drawn in master stroke

suck in the cul de sac's

diurnal rotational breeze,

the certain blond dream of the sun going down

and the gates opening up. A modesty,

the nice folks returning to nice homes, a little more tired,

no one dying miserably of too much Williams.

A willow, bay bark underneath, wet pulp

inside, twisting up to night sky.

Do you still have that project, I no longer have a project, but if you had a project

we could blow them toward one another.

Let me entertain you.

We are here to entertain.

To hold the black whips

to embroider the day of the week so as to assign it

to the towel. If it's morning, what to read, cut off, wave, tie to the emergency
    cone?

Or if you are waking in the audience, what small clearings will you make

to rest from those of us in paradises and hells

also, the ecstacies of clover sprouting near manholes

amid the thrown down tissue through which we feel

we can see it all—   The hillock, a tall oak makes a shade above it,

and propped up against the trunk

reclines a leisured figure into which we can climb back in and read

toward the tonal promises

and geographical distances connecting inside our ears at the end, the dead

dark stallions the world lets go into meadows,

the man turning into a boy

walking through those archways

as we watch, holding his hat

on a dirt road, hearing ourselves implore a strutting mystic whose trading hand

is broke. Someone adds elements to the sentences the way a girl out west

just laughs. We had lyric time, we had pylons and pylons of it,

under low lying reefs of cloud the 8 notes

necessary for infinite melody, a convective heat event.

The faces swirling, the little hands uncurling, resuscitating to stay the world
of awe.

The tiger sleeps until it is hungry, and then the tiger hunts.

NOTES AND ACKNOWLEDGMENTS

The Plot Genie takes its title from a plot-generating system created in the 1930's by Wycliffe A. Hill, a former silent screen writer. "To jump a bail bond," "a peculiar speech signal," and "to satisfy a horoscope" are from Hill's *Plot Genie: the Action and Adventure* volume. Erasures are of Jane Austen, Arthur Rimbaud, and Mark Twain. Other sources, in the order of their appearance, begin with "Drain the pond," a misprision of director Robert Bresson. "I am thy father's spirit . . ." is Hamlet. "[E and R]" owes a debt to opening lines in the film *Me and You and Everyone We Know*. Indented dialogue in "[Dear E]," is from the film *The Postman Always Rings Twice*. In "Agents of eternity . . ." the line "I was out by the fire" is from the silent classic *The Saga of Gosta Berling*. The idea of the dictionary being "a poem about everything" is from comedian Steven Wright. Page 66 is from *Plot Scientific* by Wycliffe A. Hill. Dialogue at the end of "[Redhead Leaping Over the Classic Examples to Be Born]" is from *The Man in the Grey Flannel Suit* by Sloan Wilson.

Grateful acknowledgment is made to the editors of the magazines where these poems first appeared: *American Poetry Review, A Public Space, The Canary, Carnet de Route, Colorado Review, Columbia Poetry Review, Conjunctions, Fence, Parthenon West, New American Writing, New Review of Literature, Or, Packingtown Review,* and *Verse*. The poem "The Plot Genie" appears in the anthologies *American Hybrid* (W. W. Norton) and *Lyric Postmodernisms* (Counterpath).

I would like to thank several early and crucial readers of this book: Jane Miller, Rusty Morrison, and Domenic Stansberry. Thank you, Domenic, for bringing the original Plot Genie into the house. I return it herewith. Most of all, I would like to thank the late Wycliffe A. Hill for the many journeys he has sent so many writers and readers plummeting toward, and through.

GILLIAN CONOLEY was born in 1955 in Austin, Texas, where,  on its rural outskirts, her father and mother owned and operated a radio station. She is the author of six collections of poetry, including *Profane Halo*, *Lovers in the Used World*, and *Tall Stranger*, a finalist for the National Book Critics Circle Award. Her work has received many prizes, including the Jerome J. Shestack Poetry Prize from *The American Poetry Review*, a National Endowment for the Arts grant, and a Fund for Poetry Award. She lives in the San Francisco Bay Area with her husband, novelist Domenic Stansberry, and their daughter, Gillis. Poet-in-Residence at Sonoma State University, she edits *Volt*.